KICK OFF
FOR SUCCESS
Organizing for School

About the Series Authors

Jeanette Phillips is principal of the Tenaya Middle School in Fresno, California. She has been a middle-school principal for the past 19 years and before that served as a vice-principal and as a teacher in grades K-12. Jeanette was a co-founder of the California League of Middle Schools in 1978 and continues to serve on its board as Program Chair. She was a member of the Executive Council and Board of Directors for the National Middle School Association for six years and served as the association's President in 1990–91. She received the Distinguished Service Award from the National Middle School Association in 1992, the ACSA Outstanding Educator Award and the California League of Middle Schools President's Award in 1992.

Carl Zon has been a teacher, counselor, and administrator in elementary, middle, and high schools in the states of Illinois, Wisconsin, and California. He is currently on the staff of the California League of Middle Schools and California League of High Schools. As a consultant, he has assisted schools and districts with interdisciplinary unit design and made presentations on interdisciplinary instruction as state and national conferences. He has also been a contributing author on many CLMS monographs. He is past president of the California League of Middle Schools and a recipient of the CLMS President's Award for Exceptional Service to Middle Level Education in California (1992).

About the Authors

Lisa Beadles teaches English, oral interpretation, and dance at Taft High School in Woodland, Hills, CA. She worked in Chicago's theater and corporate world before teaching and recognizes the importance of creativity, diversity, and enthusiasm as key elements to creating a motivating learning environment in the classroom for students.

Tracy Evans teaches English and oral interpretation at Taft High School, where she also sponsors the cheerleading, drill, and flag teams. She seeks to impart zeal, dedication to excellence, and a strong sense of motivation to her students.

Barbara Haskin teaches world history, educational career planning, and study skills at Taft High School, where she also coaches swimming. She is a believer in the philosophy of "teacher as coach," and recognizes the necessity of encouraging, pushing, and creating a sense of enthusiasm in students.

Carol Morgan teaches world history, educational career planning, and study skills at Taft High School. Having studied systems theory and design, she extends knowledge she has gained in those areas to curriculum design and to the interdisciplinary classroom.

Acknowledgments

Cover Design: Suzanne Schineller

Cover Photo: Rick Iwasaki/Tony Stone Images

Printed in the United States of America.

ISBN: 0-13-412537-1

10   02 01 00

TABLE OF CONTENTS

ABOUT INTERDISCIPLINARY UNITS

Successful instructional practices make strong connections between the structure and substance of subject area disciplines and the developmental characteristics of young adolescents. Interdisciplinary learning experiences are particularly appropriate for demonstrating not only the complexity, richness, and "connectedness" of knowledge but also its usefulness and application in the lives of students. Well-planned interdisciplinary units show the world operating as a whole, lend coherence to concepts otherwise isolated within specific disciplines, and empower students to use disciplines in concert and to compare and contrast them.

Kick Off for Success! Organizing for School is an interdisciplinary unit that brings together discipline-based and interdisciplinary perspectives. The unit has been designed using a step-by-step model adapted by Carl Zon and Laurie Aboudara-Robertson from the work of H. H. Jacobs (1989) and Jacobs and J. H. Borland (1986). These steps are described below.

Selecting and Defining an Organizing Center

Unit development begins with the selection of a topic or organizing center such as a theme, subject area(s), event, issue or problem. The topic needs to generate interdisciplinary exploration and be interesting and relevant to students. James Beane (1993) has defined eleven themes that express the intersection of young adolescent concerns and more global social concerns. The theme of "transitions" intersects with these categories of concerns— *understanding personal changes* and *living in a changing world*. Concepts and generalizations in state and national curriculum frameworks can also assist in unifying disciplines. Current events, including those in students' daily lives, can be particularly engaging for students.

Once a topic is chosen, teachers should explore it by using a spoked wheel as a graphic organizer. The wheel, or organizing center, includes a hub for the topic and spokes for each discipline. Teachers use brainstorming (Osborne, 1963) to define discipline-based perspectives on the chosen topic. Brainstormed associations, including concepts, generalizations, materials, and people, are written next to the related disciplinary spoke(s).

Creating a Scope-and-Sequence of Guiding Questions

The next step entails organizing the brainstormed associations and creating a scope-and-sequence of guiding questions for the unit. Brainstorming can once again be used to formulate a tentative list of questions. Students can be involved in this process.

Each guiding question should be general in nature, somewhat like a chapter heading in a textbook. The set of questions, three to six in number, must transcend disciplinary lines, flow in a logical sequence, be sensitive to time constraints, lead to answers students need to know, and be stated in language students comprehend. Study of each question should occupy about one week.

Developing Master and Individual Activity Plans

The guiding questions are now used to develop master and individual activity plans that engage students in purposeful inquiry. Bloom's Taxonomy (1956) provides a model of cognition that can guide the design of an array of activities that elicit critical and creative thinking including: knowledge acquisition, comprehension, application, analysis, synthesis, and evaluation. Master activity plans, prepared as an overview for each guiding question, summarize individual activities and list required resources.

Individual activity plans for each guiding question contain: the overall activity plan or objective; possible student groupings for the activity; Bloom's thinking process(es) highlighted in the activity; procedures for carrying out the activity; products and outcomes; standards (quality, quantity, and time); resources needed; and an evaluation scheme.

Designing an Evaluation Scheme

A comprehensive evaluation scheme is at the heart of successful interdisciplinary teaching and learning. Given the effort required to develop these experiences and the significant departure from traditional discipline-based instruction they represent, teachers must define standards meticulously and capture evidence of student growth assiduously.

Engaging activities including projects are necessary but insufficient guarantees that students benefit from interdisciplinary experiences. Effective evaluation strategies start with thoughtfully selected organizing centers, carefully stated guiding questions, and clearly defined standards and performance expectations for each activity. Students can keep journals and portfolios to document their responses to guiding questions. They can also participate in defining evaluation criteria for their products and performances.

Finally, teachers must define the value-added dimension of interdisciplinary learning by answering this critical question: "What knowledge, skills and habits of mind do we value in students as interdisciplinary learners?"Otherwise stated, teachers must design interdisciplinary experiences that provide evidence to answer these questions: What is it about interdisciplinary learning that students cannot acquire without using this approach? Are

interdisciplinary learners more likely to see connections between disciplines spontaneously? Do they draw cross-disciplinary insights more frequently? Do they use their knowledge from one discipline to strengthen their understanding of the concepts in another? Are they better synthesizers or holistic thinkers?

Heidi Hayes Jacobs has stated: "With its promise of unifying knowledge and modes of understanding, interdisciplinary education represents the pinnacle of curriculum development" (Jacobs, 1989). You are invited to the "pinnacle" of curriculum design and offered this model to assist you in meeting the interdisciplinary learning needs of adolescents.

—Carl Zon

BIBLIOGRAPHY

Beane, J. A. (1993): A middle school curriculum: From rhetoric to reality; Columbus, OH, National Middle School Association.

Bloom, B.S., ed. (1956): Taxonomy of educational objectives: The classification of educational goals, handbook 1: Cognitive domain; New York, NY, David Mckay.

Cohen, M. (November 1978): "Whatever happened to interdisciplinary education?" Educational Leadership.

Jacobs, H. H. (1989): Interdisciplinary curriculum: Design and implementation; Alexandria, VA; Association for Supervision and Curriculum Development.

Jacobs, H. H., & Borland, J. H. (Winter 1986): "The interdisciplinary concept model: Design and implementation," Gifted Child Quarterly.

Kagan, Spencer (1992) Cooperative Learning; San Juan Capistrano, CA, Kagan Cooperative Learning.

Osborn, A. F. (1963): Applied imagination; New York, NY; Charles Scribner and Company.

ABOUT THIS UNIT

"Doing school" can be an intimidating, even frightening experience for students. Balancing assignments and tests from several teachers on the same day, pacing work on projects for which there seemed to be years to complete but are suddenly due in two days, just finding one's way around a new building—these can be daunting tasks to students.

Kick Off for Success! Organizing for School is an interdisciplinary unit that will help students acquire some basic tools necessary to function in the school environment. This is a student-centered, activity-oriented, multidisciplinary unit that will help students learn not only the value of being organized but skills for working their way through assignments and projects that they can transfer to any subject area at any level of their education.

Students experience situations that point out the need for developing such skills as time management and organization of information. They discuss these skills with other students, brainstorming how such skills can best be developed and in the process developing the additional skill of cooperating with others.

The activities for the last Guiding Question present students with several different, large-scale projects that pull together the various skills they have worked with in earlier activities. With completion of these projects, students will have gained not only confidence in their abilities to handle the challenges of school but also skills that will prove useful to them outside the classroom.

This unit was developed for and has been used very successfully with high school students at-risk. The activities "personalizing" their school experience are most useful with such students. These activities can also be used successfully to orient students moving from elementary school to middle school or to junior high or moving from there to high school.

Note the information on the Master pages about teaching some of the lessons simultaneously across different disciplines or sequentially in one discipline.

INTERDISCIPLINARY WHEEL

MATH

- textbook organization

LANGUAGE ARTS

- sequencing
- journal writing
- literature analysis
- interviewing
- outlining
- oral presentations
- portfolios

SCIENCE

- textbook organization

ORGANIZING CENTER

Getting Organized for School

SOCIAL STUDIES

- timelines
- interviewing
- mapping
- researching
- writing news stories
- presenting a newscast

HEALTH/PHYSICAL EDUCATION

- textbook organization

- sequencing illustrations
- illustrating portfolios
- creating art for newscasts

THE ARTS

Source: Adapted from the work of Heidi Hayes Jacobs, 1988, by Carl Zon, Laurie Aboudara-Robertson, and the California League of Middle Schools.

Organizing Theme: Getting organized for school

Guiding questions:

1. Why do I need to be organized?

2. How do I get organized to "do school"?

3. How can I demonstrate my new organizing skills?

Source: Adapted from the work of Heidi Hayes Jacobs, 1988, by Carl Zon, Laurie Aboudara-Robertson and the Redwood Middle School, and the California League of Middle Schools.

MASTER ACTIVITY PLAN

GUIDING QUESTION 1:   Why do I need to be organized?

Activities*/Description	Math	Science	Language Arts	Social Studies	Health	The Arts	Time
1.1 Recognizing the Difficulty of Functioning in a Disorganized Environment—recognizing the difficulties that a disorganized environment can present and suggesting some of the benefits that organization can provide	✔	✔	✔	✔	✔	✔	1 class period
1.2 Analyzing Daily Activities— recognizing how students' time is used on a daily basis, completing daily schedule sheets	✔	✔	✔	✔	✔	✔	2 class periods
1.3 Understanding Time Management recognizing how time is used on a daily basis, suggesting ways to use time more effectively	✔	✔	✔	✔	✔	✔	2 class periods
1.4 Recognizing the Importance of Sequencing and Organization in Storytelling—analyzing a disorganized story for structural problems, reordering a disorganized narrative			✔			✔	1 class period
1.5 Organizing History—recognizing different ways of organizing history, organizing chronologies of personal histories				✔			1 class period

*Activities 1.1, 1.2, and 1.3 can be done simultaneously in different classes or sequentially in one class. Activities 1.4 and 1.5 can be done simultaneously.

1.1 RECOGNIZING THE DIFFICULTY OF FUNCTIONING IN A DISORGANIZED ENVIRONMENT

GUIDING QUESTION 1:   Why do I need to be organized?

SUBJECT AREAS: All

GROUPING: Whole class, individuals

MATERIALS: Classroom furnishings
Student journals or notebooks

BLOOM'S TAXONOMY LEVEL: Knowledge, Analysis

PRODUCTS AND OUTCOMES: Journal entries, chart of student responses, webs

TIME FRAME: 1 class period

Procedures:

Pre-class preparation: Before students enter the classroom, put it in disarray. Turn chairs or desks in every direction. Have no daily agenda on the chalkboard. If you have a classroom clock you can control, set it for an incorrect time. Scatter books randomly in the aisles and on table tops.

1. When students enter the classroom, ignore their responses to the disarray and announce "Let's begin" as if nothing unusual was taking place. Try to foment chaos. Call on a student as if expecting him or her to provide an answer to a previously asked question. Act as if any response is unsatisfactory, and call on another student. Issue confusing or contradictory orders. Carry on in this way for about five minutes.

2. When the five minutes are up, tell the students to write their feelings about what just went on in their notebooks or journals.

3. When students have finished writing, ask for a show of hands as to whether they thought the class opening experience was a positive or a negative situation. Chart responses on the board in a simple chart like this:

Positive	Negative

4. Now hold a classwide discussion on the opening activity. Encourage students to say *why* they thought the experience was positive or negative. Remind them, if necessary, to read the responses to the activity that they wrote down in their journals or notebooks. Have students suggest particular positives or negatives that might result from a state of disorganization. Write down their responses in a web on the chalkboard:

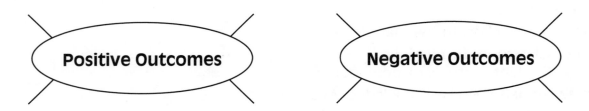

5. Close by once again polling students on their feelings about the opening activity to determine if and how their feelings on organization/disorganization have changed.

EVALUATION:
Students should be able to recognize and describe some of the difficulties of functioning in a disorganized environment.

1.2 ANALYZING DAILY ACTIVITIES

GUIDING QUESTION 1: Why do I need to be organized?

SUBJECT AREAS: All

GROUPING: Whole class, individual students

MATERIALS: One-Day Observation Sheets, 1 per student

BLOOM'S TAXONOMY LEVEL: Analysis

PRODUCTS AND OUTCOMES: Completed One-Day Observation Sheets and class computations of five leading activities and time spent on them

TIME FRAME: 2 class periods

Procedure:

Day 1

1. Divide the class into small cooperative groups. Ask groups to work together to determine how each member spent the previous day. Tell them to try to remember all their various activities that day and to estimate how long they spent on each one. Have the groups make lists of their activities and the time spent on them.

2. Have the groups compare their lists. Which activities occupied the most time? Which the least? Work with students to compute the average time spent each day on the five activities that occupied the most time.

3. Distribute One-Day Observation sheets to each student. Explain that understanding how time is used is an important first step to managing it well. Earlier in the class, students gave their impressions of how they used their time. Now they'll have a chance to check the accuracy of those impressions by completing the Observation Sheets. Tell them to keep track of their activities for one day by answering the questions on the sheet.

Day 2

1. After students have had a full day to complete their activity sheets, have them form into the same groups as on Day 1 to review their Observation Sheets. Do students note any differences between their initial impressions of how they spent their time and their actual observations?

2. Have students reassemble and decide which five activities occupied the most time and compute the average time spent on them. Were there any differences from their earlier observations?

EVALUATION:

Students should be able to complete Observation Sheets and to recognize how they use their time during the course of a day.

ONE-DAY OBSERVATION SHEET

Keep track of your activities for one day by filling in the blanks below.

1. I got up this morning at _____

2. Getting ready for school took me (how long?) _____

3. Eating breakfast took me (how long?) _____

4. Getting to school took me (how long?) _____

5. I spent the following amounts of time in each of my classes: _____

Subject: _____ Time: _____   Subject: _____ Time: _____

Subject: _____ Time: _____   Subject: _____ Time: _____

Subject: _____ Time: _____   Subject: _____ Time: _____

Subject: _____ Time: _____   Subject: _____ Time: _____

6. Eating lunch took me (how long?) _____

7. Other activities at school were these (give activity and time spent):

_____

_____

_____

_____

8. Getting home from school took me (how long?) _____

9. Eating dinner took me (how long?) _____

10. Other things I did today were these (give activity and time spent):

_____

_____

_____

_____

11. I went to bed this evening at _____

12. I (circle one) did/ did not have time to do everything I had to do today. Explain your answer.

_____

_____

_____

_____

1.3 UNDERSTANDING TIME MANAGEMENT

GUIDING QUESTION 1:   Why do I need to be organized?

SUBJECT AREAS: All
GROUPING: Whole class, pairs of students
MATERIALS: A Day in the Life and Time Management sheets, 1 per student
BLOOM'S TAXONOMY LEVEL: Knowledge, Analysis, Interpretation
PRODUCTS AND OUTCOMES: Completed A Day in the Life and Time Management sheets, master list of time management suggestions
TIME FRAME: 2 class periods

Procedure:

Day 1

1. Write the words *Time* and *Organization* on the chalkboard. Ask students to quickwrite in their journals or notebooks about how they think the two words are associated.

2. When students have had a chance to complete their writing, hold a class discussion on the relationship between the words. Help students to understand, through the discussion, that organizing time is an important factor in organizing anything, from one's study schedule to one's performance in a job.

3. Tell students that, in order to learn more about organizing and managing their time, they should first take a closer look at how they spend it. Distribute Day in the Life sheets to each student. Tell them that, beginning tomorrow, they should keep a complete record of the day's activities, writing down the time they begin each new activity.

Day 2

1. After students have had a full day to complete their activity sheets, distribute Time Management sheets to each student. Tell them to review their Day in the Life sheets and write down on the Time Management sheets any activities in which they felt they were wasting time or not using time efficiently.

2. Divide the class into a number of cooperative groups. Have students in each group compare their Time Management sheets to look for common areas where they had problems with using time efficiently. Tell each group to develop two general suggestions for managing time more efficiently.

9

3. Allow each group to present its suggestions to the class as a whole. Record the suggestions on a master list on the chalkboard. Then open a general discussion on the suggestions. Suggest that students edit out or combine suggestions that seem to duplicate each other. Encourage students to offer ways that various suggestions could be improved. Ask if the list suggests other ways to use time more efficiently. When students have arrived at a final list, have them copy it into their notebooks or journals.

EVALUATION:
Students should be able to analyze their own use of time and suggest ways of improving their use of it for a master time management list.

A DAY IN THE LIFE

Fill out the chart below as you go through the day. From the time you get up in the morning until you go to bed at night, every time you begin a new activity, note the time and what you are doing on the chart.* For example:

6 A.M.	Wake up and make bed.
6:15 A.M.	Eat breakfast.
6:30 A.M.	Wash breakfast dishes

Time (AM/PM)	Activity	Time (AM/PM)	Activity

*Use the back of this sheet if you run out of space above.

TIME MANAGEMENT

Look back on the day you described in your A Day in the Life sheet. Were there points at which you felt you were wasting time or not using it as well as you could. Fill out the chart below describing those points and why the time wasn't being well used.

Activity/Time	Why Time Wasn't Used Well

Looking back on your day, describe things you might do to help you use your time better in the future.

_____

_____

_____

_____

_____

_____

_____

_____

_____

_____

1.4 RECOGNIZING THE IMPORTANCE OF SEQUENCING AND ORGANIZATION IN STORYTELLING

GUIDING QUESTION 1:   Why do I need to be organized?

SUBJECT AREAS: Language Arts, the Arts

GROUPING: Whole class, cooperative groups

MATERIALS: Short stories, folk tales, comic books or comic strips
Student journals or notebooks

BLOOM'S TAXONOMY LEVEL: Analysis

PRODUCTS AND OUTCOMES: Resequenced stories or comic strips, journal entries

TIME FRAME: 1 class period

Procedure:

Pre-class preparation: Select a relatively brief short story or folk tale. Make a photocopy of it, then cut it up into segments of differing length and rearrange them, disrupting the story's original sequence. This will be your reading copy.

Then prepare copies of different disarranged stories or tales for student work groups. For these disarranged stories, be sure each resequenced paragraph or cluster of paragraphs is on a separate sheet of paper, and number each sheet consecutively in the disarranged order. Make as many copies of the disarranged story as you will have student work groups.

Alternatively or additionally, you might cut up panels from a comic strip or comic book episode, rearrange them, and photocopy them for student work groups.

1. Begin the class by reading aloud your prepared, disarranged story to the students.
2. When you are done, elicit the students' responses to the story by asking questions like these: What happened in the story? Could you follow it? Did it make sense?

3. After students have had a chance to give their initial responses, lead a discussion on the importance of sequencing and organization in story telling. Point out how having a recognizable structure and sequence help readers or listeners keep track of who's who in a story, who did what, and the relationships among events in the story. Ask students to suggest ways they might have changed the order of events in the story you read to make it more understandable. Record their suggestions, then reread the story taking their suggestions into account.

4. Then divide the class into small cooperative groups. Give each group a copy of the disarranged story you have prepared. Tell the groups to rearrange the order of the story into a sequence that they think tells the story most effectively. When they are finished, they should write down the page numbers showing the new order of the story.

5. When all groups are done, ask volunteers from each group to write the page numbers of the story in the order that their group has decided upon on the chalkboard. Allow groups to compare the selected orderings and discuss any variations in them.

6. Conclude the activity by having students write brief entries in their journals or notebooks on the importance of organization and sequencing to storytelling.

EVALUATION:
Students should be able to recognize the importance of sequencing and organization to story structure and be able to arrange disordered narratives in a more comprehensible and effective fashion.

1.5 ORGANIZING HISTORY

GUIDING QUESTION 1:   Why do I need to be organized?

SUBJECT AREAS: Social Studies

GROUPING: Whole class, individual students

BLOOM'S TAXONOMY LEVEL: Knowledge, Application, Synthesis, Comprehension, Analysis

PRODUCTS AND OUTCOMES: Completed Personal History Timelines

TIME FRAME: 1 class periods

Procedure:

1. Write the word *history* on the chalkboard. Have students brainstorm the different ways history can be arranged or organized. Possible responses might include: events, people, artifacts, timelines, etc. If students need more ideas, have them skim through their social studies textbooks or any other books in the class resource center. Write student repsonses on the chalkboard.

2. Now write *chronology* on the chalkboard. Tell them that this word comes from two Greek words, *chronos* meaning "time" and *logia* meaning "a collection." Based on these two meanings, what do students think a chronology is? (an order of things by the dates on which they occurred) Ask students to suggest 15 items that might be included in a chronology of major events in U.S. history. Write down their suggestions, then have students use history books or encyclopedias to confirm the dates of the events and have students write the events in chronological order on separate sheets of paper. When students are done, have them call out the events in order and write them as a master list on the chalkboard.

3. Ask students to suggest events that might appear on a chronolgy of their own lives. Possible responses might include birth, any births or deaths of family members, any changes in residence, changes in schools, trips, etc.

4. *Assignment:* Tell students that they should now attempt to organize the events of their own lives in the form of Personal History Timelines. Explain that they can use any combinations of dates, pictures, and words to create chronological accounts of the events that were important in their own lives. When students have completed the assignment, you can ask if any volunteers wish to share their timelines with the class by posting them on the bulletin board.

EVALUATION:

Students should be able to explain different ways in which history is organized and create chronologies of their personal histories.

MASTER ACTIVITY PLAN

GUIDING QUESTION 2: How do I get organized to "do school"?

Activities*/Description	Math	Science	Language Arts	Social Studies	Health	The Arts	Time
2.1 Making an Organizational Notebook—understanding how a structured notebook can help structure time and activities	✔	✔	✔	✔	✔	✔	1 class period
2.2 Personalizing School—Meeting the People—familiarizing students with the organization of their school				✔			at least 2 class periods
2.3 Personalizing School—Understanding the Landscape—recognizing the physical layout of the school plant and important landmarks in it				✔			2 class periods
2.4 Understanding Textbook Organization—recognizing the components of a textbook and their purposes	✔	✔	✔	✔	✔	✔	1 class period
2.5 Organizing the School Year—recognizing major events in the school year; making a calendar	✔	✔	✔	✔	✔	✔	3 class periods
2.6 Organizing for a Large Research Project—planning and scheduling a long-term activity	✔	✔	✔	✔	✔	✔	1 class period
2.7 Organizing an Interview and an Introduction—developing questioning strategies; practicing the organization of information			✔	✔			3 class periods
2.8 Organizing to Research Study Strategies—developing questioning strategies	✔	✔	✔	✔	✔	✔	1 class period

*Activities 2.1, 2.2, and 2.3 and Activities 2.6, 2.7 and 2.8 can be done simultaneously.

2.1 MAKING AN ORGANIZATIONAL NOTEBOOK

GUIDING QUESTION 2: How do I get organized to "do school"?

SUBJECT AREAS: All

GROUPING: Whole class, cooperative groups, individual students

MATERIALS: Student notebooks
Notebook materials such as dividers, tabs, etc.
Identification Data sheet, 1 per student
Class Schedule sheet, 1 per student
Assignment sheet, 1 per student

BLOOM'S TAXONOMY LEVEL: Analysis, knowledge, application

PRODUCTS AND OUTCOMES: Organized student notebooks

TIME FRAME: 1 class period

Procedure:

1. Divide the class into cooperative work groups. Ask the groups to think about how a well-organized notebook could help them be better organized for school. Ask each group to brainstorm ideas of things that a well-organized notebook might contain. Tell each group to arrive at a master list of five items.

2. When groups are done, have them present their master lists to the class as a whole. Have a whole class discussion on the items suggested with the aim of arriving at a mutually agreed-upon master list of about 10 items. You might, during the discussion, project examples of the Class Schedule sheets and the Student I.D. and Daily Reminder sheets and ask students if they think similar items would be helpful.

3. Make notebook materials listed above available and allow students time to create their own organized notebooks.

4. Review student notebooks and allow volunteers to explain their organizational schemes.

EVALUATION:

Students should be able to list elements that would contribute to a well-organized notebook and create such a notebook for themselves.

IDENTIFICATION DATA

SCHOOL NAME _____

STUDENT NAME _____

ADDRESS _____

PHONE NUMBER _____

IN CASE OF EMERGENCY, CALL _____

LOCKER NUMBER _____   HOMEROOM _____

REMEMBER TO ALWAYS CHECK THE FOLLOWING

LEAVING HOME:

☑ Do I have all the books I need for school today?

☑ Do I have all assignments that are due today?

☑ Do I have everything else I need for school today—

    lunch?   lunch money?   gym clothes?   bus pass?

AT SCHOOL:

☑ Have I written down all class assignments, including pages to read,

    questions to answer, and date the assignment is due,

    on my Assignments calendar?

☑ Have I written down the date of any upcoming tests

    on my Assignments calendar?

LEAVING SCHOOL:

☑ Do I have all the books I will need tonight?

☑ Do I have all my homework assignments?

☑ Do I have all the materials I'll need to complete my assignments?

☑ Do I need to bring anything else home tonight?

☑ Do I have to stop at the library or anyplace else on the way home?

CLASS SCHEDULE

PERIOD	TIME	CLASS	TEACHER	ROOM
1				
2				
3				
4				
5				
6				
7				
8				

CLASS SCHEDULE

PERIOD	TIME	CLASS	TEACHER	ROOM
1				
2				
3				
4				
5				
6				
7				
8				

CLASS SCHEDULE

PERIOD	TIME	CLASS	TEACHER	ROOM
1				
2				
3				
4				
5				
6				
7				
8				

CLASS SCHEDULE

PERIOD	TIME	CLASS	TEACHER	ROOM
1				
2				
3				
4				
5				
6				
7				
8				

ASSIGNMENTS FOR (MONTH) _____

Monday	Tuesday	Wednesday	Thursday	Friday

Use the following abbreviations when filling out the assignment schedule:

Art
F.L.=Foreign Language
Hth.=Health

H.E.=Home Economics
Hist.=History
LA=Language Arts

Math=Mathematics
Mu=Music
Read.=Reading

Sci.=Science
S.S.=Social Studies

2.2 PERSONALIZING SCHOOL—MEETING THE PEOPLE

GUIDING QUESTION 2:   How do I get organized to "do school"?

SUBJECT AREAS: Social Studies

GROUPING: Whole class, individuals

MATERIALS: Who's Who sheets, one per student
Student handbooks or school organizational charts

BLOOM'S TAXONOMY LEVEL: Knowledge

PRODUCTS AND OUTCOMES: Completed Who's Who sheets

TIME FRAME: At least 2 class periods

Procedure:

Pre-class preparation: Study the Who's Who sheet accompanying this activity. Use an asterisk or some other mark to indicate which positions exist in your school for students to investigate. In the blank spaces, add any additional positions you feel are appropriate. Then make photocopies of the amended sheet.

Then, invite as many of the personnel listed on the sheet as possible to visit the class for brief question-and-answer sessions with students. Having several people visit during one class session would be ideal, but because of their schedules you may have to spread visits out over a few periods. Ask the visitors to prepare brief introductory statements explaining their roles in the school. If some personnel cannot visit the classroom, arrange for students to visit them at their workplaces.

Period 1

1. Draw the following diagram on the chalkboard:

Ask students to brainstorm other people and positions who are important in the running of the school. Ask students who suggest names or positions to briefly explain what roles those people or positions play in the operation of the school. Add the suggestions to the diagram on the board.

2. Distribute copies of the Who's Who sheet as it applies to your school to all students. Then divide the class into cooperative groups and have them work together to fill in names for each of the positions indicated on the sheets. Students may use student handbooks or school organizational charts to complete their sheets.

3. When groups have completed their sheets, check the accuracy of their work by calling on the groups in turn to give the names associated with the positions.

4. Then tell the groups to think of one question to ask each of the people listed on the sheet about his or her job. They should write their questions in the places provided on the Who's Who sheet. Review the questions for appropriateness before the personnel visit.

Period 2 and after

1. The school personnel you have invited should visit the class and give their brief statements about their jobs. You should then open a question-and-answer session with students asking the questions on their Who's Who sheets. Students should write the answers in the spaces provided.

2. For those personnel who cannot come to class, have students visit them at their workplaces. Students can ask their questions there and get the personnel to initial the Who's Who sheet to show that the visit was made.

EVALUATION:
Students should be able to give the names of key school personnel and explain what roles those people play in the operation of the school.

WHO'S WHO

Fill in the names of the people in your school who hold the positions listed below. Think of a question you would like to ask each person about his or her position. Write your questions in the spaces provided. When you have a chance to ask your questions, write their answers on a separate sheet of paper or on the back of this sheet. If you visit any of the listed personnel at their workplaces to ask your question, have them initial your sheet next to their names.

Position	Name of Person	Question
Principal		
Assistant Principal		
Head Counselor		
Dean		
College Adviser		
Career Adviser		
Plant Manager		
Cafeteria Head		
Nurse		
Media Resource Head		
Counselor		
Class Adviser		

2.3 PERSONALIZING SCHOOL— UNDERSTANDING THE LANDSCAPE

GUIDING QUESTION 2:   How do I get organized to "do school"?

SUBJECT AREAS: Social Studies

GROUPING: Whole class, student pairs

MATERIALS: A variety of street maps and building plans
Opaque projector

BLOOM'S TAXONOMY LEVEL: Knowledge, Synthesis

PRODUCTS AND OUTCOMES: Student maps and directions

TIME FRAME: 2 class periods

Procedure:

Period 1

1. Display the wall maps and building plans you have assembled. Review basics of map reading with students, making sure that they understand basic directions such as north, south, east, west, right, and left. You may also wish to review map scales. Using the opaque projector, display a segment of a road map to the class. Using a pointer, trace out a route on the map as volunteers call out descriptions of your route; for example, "You're going north up Main St." "Now you're turning right on Maple Ave." "You're turning right and going west on Auburn St."

2. Divide the class into pairs. Then display another segment of a street map or building plan with an *X* and a *Y* marking two separate locations. Tell pairs to work together to write directions on how to get from *X* to *Y*.

3. After student pairs are done, call on volunteers to read their directions to the rest of the class. Have students vote on which route is the best.

4. Tell the student pairs that they are now to write directions of how to get to important places in the school. Assign each pair a position listed in the Who's Who sheet for Activity 2.1. The pairs are to write out how to get from the classroom to the office or workplace of the person holding that position. Student pairs may also draw maps of their routes.

Period 2

Have pairs swap directions and give students time to critique and correct the routes. Ask volunteers to read their descriptions or display their maps to the class as a whole.

EVALUATION:

Students should be able to describe how to get from their classroom to important places throughout the school building.

2.4 UNDERSTANDING TEXTBOOK ORGANIZATION

GUIDING QUESTION 2:   How do I get organized to "do school"?

SUBJECT AREAS: All

GROUPING: Whole class, cooperative groups

MATERIALS: Student textbooks

BLOOM'S TAXONOMY LEVEL: Knowledge

PRODUCTS AND OUTCOMES: Oral reports on textbook organization

TIME FRAME: 1 class period

Procedure:

1. Divide the class into cooperative work groups. Tell the groups that their task is to analyze the structure and organization of the textbook used in this class. You may suggest that each group assign responsibilities for explaining a different part of the text to different students; for example, the front matter of the book to one student; any special features in the text to another; the text itself, including its division into parts, units, chapters and so forth, to a third; any questions in the text to a fourth, and so on. Other areas that you should alert students to consider in analyzing their texts include use of illustrations—photos, maps, charts, diagrams, etc.; treatment of new vocabulary; and back matter, including glossaries, atlases, appendices, indices, etc.

2. Each group should present its report to the class as a whole, allowing time at the end of each presentation for questions and critiques.

3. Then hold a whole class discussion in which students try to reach consensus on a one-sentence statement about how each part of the book makes studying easier or more effective.

EVALUATION:

Students should be able to understand and explain the various parts of their textbook.

2.5 ORGANIZING THE SCHOOL YEAR

GUIDING QUESTION 2:   How do I get organized to "do school"?

SUBJECT AREAS: All

GROUPING: Whole class, cooperative groups

MATERIALS: Sheets of poster board, one for each month of the school year and other supplies for making calendars including felt-tipped markers of various colors, sheets of different colored construction paper, rulers, scissors, glue, and staplers.

BLOOM'S TAXONOMY LEVEL: Analysis, Synthesis, Application

PRODUCTS AND OUTCOMES: School year calendars

TIME FRAME: 3 class periods

Procedure:

Pre-class preparation: Before students come into the classroom, write on the chalkboard a list of important school dates for the coming year. Include school holidays, report card days, major school assembly days, etc.

Period 1

1. Begin the class by pointing out your chalkboard list. Tell students that these are just some of the significant dates that will be coming up in the next school year. Ask students to suggest other important dates. Have volunteers act as recorders and write down student suggestions. Remember to ask if any students have birthdays during the upcoming school year. The recorders should write down those dates as well.

2. When all suggestions and dates have been listed, tell students that one way of organizing all this data is to make an illustrated calendar of the school year. Divide the class into cooperative work groups, one for each month of the school year.

Each group is to make a poster-sized calendar of its month. Events from the chalkboard list that fall into a group's month should be on the calendar; in addition, students may brainstorm or research in almanacs or encyclopedias other dates to highlight in their month. For example, September is Hispanic Heritage Month; February is Black Heritage Month; March is Women's History Month. The events can be indicated with a label on the appropriate date or students may choose to create some artwork or clip pictures from a magazine to illustrate the event. Tell students they should also think of a graphic icon that will serve as a theme for their month.

3. Tell students to begin to research and discuss ideas for their calendars. Tell them they should create rough sketches before beginning to work on the poster board. As students work on their ideas, circulate to each group, making sure that students have the correct number of days in their month and that the days the month begins and ends are correct.

Period 2

1. Groups should finalize their rough drafts.
2. Once you have given your approval, work can begin on the final versions of the monthly calendar.

Period 3

When all months are done, each group should present and explain its creation. If there is room to display all months simultaneously, do so; otherwise, display one at a time, changing the posters as the months change.

EVALUATION:

Students should be able to recognize significant events in the school year and organize those dates in the form of monthly calendars.

2.6 ORGANIZING FOR A LARGE RESEARCH PROJECT

GUIDING QUESTION 2: How do I get organized to "do school"?

SUBJECT AREAS: All

GROUPING: Whole class, individual students

MATERIALS: Pile of books or other objects, plus a sheet or other covering for them

Who I Am Portfolio Assignment sheets, 1 per student

Who I Am Project Tracking sheets, 1 per student

BLOOM'S TAXONOMY LEVEL: Analysis, Knowledge, Application

PRODUCTS AND OUTCOMES: Completed Project Tracking sheets

TIME FRAME: 1 class period

Procedure:

Pre-class preparation: Before class, make a pile of books or other objects too large for one student to move and cover it with a sheet.

1. Tell students that you will be giving them an assignment to plan, design, and create a portfolio at least 15 pages long. Ask students to write their feelings about such a large assignment in their notebooks or journals.

2. When students are done writing, ask volunteers to share their feelings about such a project. Encourage students to express any fears or wishes to procrastinate they may have in the face of a large project.

3. Then point out the covered pile at the front of the class. Ask if anyone can move the pile to the other side of the classroom all at once by him or herself. Students will probably admit they can't. Then remove the cover. Ask students if they can think of other ways to move the materials. Students should suggest moving a few objects at a time.

4. Point out that, just as breaking the large pile down into smaller pieces made it movable, breaking a large research project into smaller pieces also makes it "do-able." Then distribute the Portfolio Assignment sheets to the students. Explain that their research project will be to create "Who I Am" portfolios, following the basic outline provided on the sheet. Ask students into what pieces this large project could be broken up. (individual pages)

5. Remind students that another important element in finishing a large project is organizing the time to work on it. Distribute Project Tracking sheets to the students. Hold a whole class discussion in which students decide how long the entire project should take and set interim dates for each piece of the portfolio as well as a final date for completed projects.

EVALUATION:

Students should be able to recognize the advantages of breaking a large research project down into smaller component parts.

Students should be able to collectively set project schedules and deadlines.

WHO I AM PORTFOLIO ASSIGNMENT

Your assignment is to create a portfolio that tells people about who you are. The contents can include your writings, passages from writings by other people, your drawings, your photographs or illustrations from newspapers or magazines, or any other materials that will fit into the portfolio pages and help explain who you are. The portfolio can have as many pages as you wish, but it must have at least one page for every part listed below. Remember, you can use words or drawings when the directions below ask you to describe some part of your life.

Cover	Create your own design. Be sure to include your name, class, period, and the date the portfolio is finished.
Table of Contents	List the titles of each page of the portfolio and the pages on which they fall. You may wish to illustrate the titles.
Here I Am	Include a picture of yourself.
Vital Data	Give your date of birth, your age, and a general physical description of yourself.
My People	Describe members of your family and/or other people who are important to you.
My Heritage	Talk with family members or do library research and tell something of your national or ethnic background.
Who I Am	Describe how you see your personality. Say why you react to situations, people, and things as you do.
What I Do	Describe some of the activities or areas in which you feel you are most successful.
My Favorite Things	Describe your favorites in music, television, movies, sports, and other areas. Explain why they are favorites.
Changing	Describe ways in which you would like to grow or change over the next 10 years.
Steps to Change	Describe steps that you could take that might help you to change in the ways you want.
Tomorrow	Imagine that it is 20 years from today. Write a letter to a friend describing your life up to this point.

WHO I AM PORTFOLIO PROJECT TRACKING

Title of Project: _____

Final Deadline: _____

Total Days to Final Deadline: _____

Materials Needed: _____

_____

PORTFOLIO TRACKING CHART		
Portfolio Section	**Deadline**	**Completed (✓)**
Completed Portfolio		

2.7 ORGANIZING AN INTERVIEW AND AN INTRODUCTION

GUIDING QUESTION 2: How do I get organized to "do school"?

SUBJECT AREAS: Language Arts, Social Studies

GROUPING: Whole class, student pairs, individual students

BLOOM'S TAXONOMY LEVEL: Analysis, Comprehension, Application

PRODUCTS AND OUTCOMES: Completed introductory speeches

TIME FRAME: 3 class periods

Procedure:

Period 1

1. Ask students to think of a topic they would like to tell the class more about and write their topics on a piece of paper. Divide the class into pairs either at random or by teaming students you think will work well together.

2. Inform student pairs that they are to take turns interviewing each other about their topics. The purpose of the interviews is to gather enough information so that each student in the pair will be able to give a spoken introduction to a presentation of the other's topic.

   Remind students that an introduction should grab the audience's attention and make them want to learn more about the topic. The introduction should also give them some information about the topic, so that they will feel they can relate to the topic. Finally, the introduction should tell them something about the person who will be delivering the presentation and why the audience should listen to him or her speak about the topic.

   Tell students to gather this information by asking questions and taking notes. Remind students that reporters use the 5 Ws and H—Who? What? When? Where? Why? and How?—when interviewing subjects. Sample questions might include: Who first told you about this topic? What would you like people to know about this topic? When did you get interested in the topic? Where can people find out more about the topic? Questions like this can help make the topic more personal and human and provide an "angle" for the introduction and the presentation that would follow.

3. Allow students to conduct their interviews and work on their introductions for the rest of the period.

Periods 2 and 3

Over the next two class periods, allow students to present their introductions to the class. When each introductory speech is complete, the other students will critique it, analyzing its content and the speaker's delivery of it.

EVALUATION:

Students should be able to interview peers and gather enough information to deliver effective oral introductions to peer presentations.

2.8 ORGANIZING TO RESEARCH STUDY STRATEGIES

GUIDING QUESTION 2:   How do I get organized to "do school"?

SUBJECT AREAS: All

GROUPING: Whole class, cooperative groups

BLOOM'S TAXONOMY LEVEL: Analysis, Comprehension, Application

PRODUCTS AND OUTCOMES: Completed lists of questions

TIME FRAME: 1 class period

Procedure:

1. Tell students that in this activity they are going to play the roles of reporters who are seeking to discover the secrets of more effective strategies for studying. Remind them of the basic questioning words that reporters use when investigating a story. They are known as the 5Ws and H for Who? What? When? Where? Why? and How? Point out that asking questions beginning with these words can help reporters, and students, explore many different facets of a problem or question.

2. Divide the class into a number of cooperative groups. Tell students within each group that they are to develop questions to ask of teachers, counselors, librarians, and students the answers to which would help build more effective ways of studying. Tell each student group to develop one master question—How can the school library be used most effectively when studying—and then ask 5Ws and H questions that explore different aspects of the master question. Each group should record its master question and its related questions as well as the names of the people to whom the questions would be addressed.

3. When groups have had adequate time to complete their questions, have groups present them to the class as a whole. Other students can critique the questions or suggest additional ones.

EVALUATION:

Students should be able to develop investigative questions using the 5Ws and H methodology.

GUIDING QUESTION 3: How can I demonstrate my new organizing skills?

Activities/Description	Math	Science	Language Arts	Social Studies	Health	The Arts	Time
3.1 Analyzing and Critiquing Student Projects—providing constructive criticism of other students' projects, incorporating other students' criticisms into one's own project	✔	✔	✔	✔	✔	✔	1 class period, plus time for student revision of projects
3.2 Presenting Portfolios—Oral Presentation—planning an oral presentation of student projects to the class			✔				3 to 4 class periods
3.3 Presenting Portfolios—Preparing an Exhibition—planning a display of student projects to an invited audience			✔				3 to 4 class periods
3.4 Organizing a Presentation of Literature—orally introducing and interpreting a work of literature, evaluating student performances			✔				3 to 4 class periods
3.5 Organizing a Newscast Project—analyzing the structure of a televised newscast, planning and scheduling a student newscast, researching and writing news stories and supporting materials				✔			3 class periods
3.6 Presenting a Student Newscast—organizing and coordinating the elements of a large project, editing and writing news stories and supporting materials, performing in a newscast				✔			3 class periods

*Page 42 consists of an Evaluation Sheet that should be distributed to students after completion of the three major projects—the portfolio exhibition, the literature presentation, and the student newscast—described under Guiding Question 3. Student responses will help determine how well they understand the organizational skills they have developed in the course of this unit.

3.1 ANALYZING AND CRITIQUING STUDENT PROJECTS

GUIDING QUESTION 3: How can I demonstrate my new organizing skills?

SUBJECT AREAS: All

GROUPING: Whole class, cooperative groups

MATERIALS: Student Who I Am portfolios

BLOOM'S TAXONOMY LEVEL: Analysis, Synthesis, Evaluation

PRODUCTS AND OUTCOMES: Written critiques of Who I Am portfolios, master list of portfolio strengths and weaknesses

TIME FRAME: 1 class period plus time for portfolio revision

Procedure:

1. Divide the class into a number of small cooperative groups. Distribute several first draft Who I Am portfolios to each group. Before doing so, attach a sheet or sheets of paper to the back of each portfolio.

2. Tell students in their groups to each read a portfolio carefully. Students should then write on the attached sheet of paper three strong qualities the portfolio displays as well as three areas in which it might be improved. When a student has finished critiquing a portfolio, he or she should pass it along to another member of the group and read and critique another portfolio. Students should keep passing around portfolios until all members of their group have had a chance to critique each portfolio.

3. Each group should then brainstorm a basic list of three of the best qualities and three of the most serious problems that the portfolios read by their group displayed.

4. When all groups are done with the tasks above, hold a general class discussion on the portfolio strengths and weaknesses, having volunteer recorders make a master list of the criteria for a good portfolio on the chalkboard.

5. Return the critiqued portfolios to their creators and allow them time to revise or edit their portfolios based on the written comments and the class discussion of portfolio strengths and weaknesses.

EVALUATION:

Students should be able to analyze the work of classmates and offer suggestions for improving it.

Students should be able to use criticism of their peers to improve their own work and self-reflection skills.

3.2 PRESENTING PORTFOLIOS—ORAL PRESENTATION

GUIDING QUESTION 3: How can I demonstrate my new organizing skills?

SUBJECT AREAS: Language Arts

GROUPING: Whole class, individual students

MATERIALS: Student Who I Am portfolios
Video camera for taping (optional)

BLOOM'S TAXONOMY LEVEL: Analysis, Synthesis, Evaluation

PRODUCTS AND OUTCOMES: Lists of presentation points, written critiques of Who I Am portfolio presentations

TIME FRAME: 3-4 class periods

Procedure:

Period 1

1. After students have had a chance to complete revisions of their Who I Am portfolios, tell them they should now think about how to present those portfolios to the public. Inform them that their first presentations will be oral ones to other members of the class. Have the students brainstorm what should be included in student presentations of their portfolios. You might suggest, as a way of starting the discussion and focusing the presentations, that student presenters highlight one area of the portfolio about which they care most deeply. You might also suggest that students choose at least one piece of artwork from their portfolios to display and talk about. Record other student suggestions on the chalkboard. Then have students work to reach consensus on five major things to be included in each presentation.

2. Allow students time to plan their presentations.

Periods 2-4

1. Students should begin to give their presentations. If equipment is available, you might want to videotape the presentations.

2. After each presentation, students should applaud the presenter, then write critiques of the effort. Critiques should take into account such factors as the portfolio content, how well the presenter covered points the class agreed on in the first period, and overall performance, including vocal projection and physical gestures.

EVALUATION:

Students should be able to list key criteria for oral presentations.

Students should be able to make effective oral presentations of their portfolios.

3.3 PRESENTING PORTFOLIOS—PREPARING AN EXHIBITION

GUIDING QUESTION 3: How can I demonstrate my new organizing skills?

SUBJECT AREAS: Language Arts

GROUPING: Whole class, cooperative groups

MATERIALS: Who I Am portfolios
Materials for exhibiting portfolios will vary depending upon the complexity of presentation you and the students decide on

BLOOM'S TAXONOMY LEVEL: Analysis, Synthesis, Evaluation

PRODUCTS AND OUTCOMES: Plan for organizing the presentation, schedules for exhibition committees, exhibition of Who I Am portfolios

TIME FRAME: 3-4 class periods

Procedure:

Pre-class preparation: Arrange for space in the school library or some other suitable area to hold an exhibition of the students' Who I Am portfolios. Part of the exhibition will be an "opening," like that of an art show at a gallery to which guests are invited and at which light refreshments are served. Begin planning at least a month before the actual exhibition. (Note that preparation activities can overlap with the students' preparation of their portfolios.)

Period 1

1. Announce that an important part of the Who I Am portfolio project is the organization of an exhibition of the portfolios for the general public, including other students, school faculty, and parents. Describe what a gallery opening is like, then set a date for the opening of the exhibition. Ask students to brainstorm how to get ready for the exhibition. Help them to see that the same principle of breaking a large task down into smaller pieces applies here as it did in the preparation of the portfolios. In this case, assigning tasks to committees will help break organization of the exhibition into manageable chunks. Among possible committees into which students might be divided are those for set-up, programming, invitations, refreshments, and clean-up, or any others you and the students find appropriate.

2. Divide the students into their committees. Let each committee set a schedule, with interim deadlines, for the work it must do.

3. Either the class as a whole or representatives of all the committees should meet to ensure that committee schedules are properly coordinated. Have volunteers create a master timetable on which the progress of the committees toward the final deadline can be recorded.

Following Periods

Students should meet as necessary to carry out the tasks of their committees. Progress should be recorded on the master timetable. The activity culminates in the exhibition of portfolios arranged according to student plan. At the formal "opening," invited guests will browse through portfolio displays, enjoy refreshments, and watch students present highlights from the many different portfolios. After the opening, the portfolios will remain on exhibit for whatever period you have arranged.

EVALUATION:

Students should be able to make plans and set schedules for a complex, long-term project.

Students should be able to carry out assigned tasks as committee members.

Students should be able to present their portfolios to an invited audience.

3.4 ORGANIZING A PRESENTATION OF LITERATURE

GUIDING QUESTION 3: How can I demonstrate my new organizing skills?

SUBJECT AREAS: Language Arts

GROUPING: Whole class, individual students

MATERIALS: Student literature selections
Evaluating the Presentation sheets, enough copies for
students to evaluate all presenters

BLOOM'S TAXONOMY LEVEL: Analysis, Application, Synthesis, Evaluation

PRODUCTS AND OUTCOMES: Student presentations; completed Evaluating
the Presentation sheets for each performance

TIME FRAME: 3-4 class periods

Procedure:

Period 1

1. Tell students that they are to plan the presentation of a favorite piece of literature to the class. They are to prepare an introduction for the work explaining why they like it, what the work says to them, and why other people should be interested in it. (Remind them of what they learned about introductions in Activity 2.7.) They will then give a reading of a poem, essay, short story, play, or novel. Tell them that if their favorite is a longer work, they should read a representative selection from the work rather than the whole thing. After they have read the selection, they should create an appropriate conclusion to their presentation. Tell students that their entire performances should be from 5 to 10 minutes in length. You may wish to give a sample presentation yourself at this time as a model.

2. Allow students to spend the rest of the period thinking about their selections and planning their performances.

Following Periods

1. Distribute Evaluating the Performance sheets to the class. Each student should receive enough sheets to evaluate that period's presentations.

2. Have students to make their presentations.

3. Allow enough time after each presentation for students to complete the evaluation sheets.

EVALUATION:

Students should be able to organize and perform a presentation of a favorite work of literature.

Students should be able to evaluate the performances of their peers.

EVALUATING THE PERFORMANCE

Study this sheet before your classmates begin their performances so you will know what points to consider in evaluating their efforts. After the performance, give your rating by making a check in the appropriate box. A "1" is the highest mark in each category and a "5" is the lowest. You may write addition comments about the performance on the back of this sheet.

Name of Presenter _____

Name of Work Presented _____

Introduction

	1	2	3	4	5
Effectiveness at grabbing and hold the audience					
Effectiveness at setting the mood and tone of the work					
Effectiveness at giving information about the author and the work					

Performance of the Selection

	1	2	3	4	5
Speaking clearly and loudly enough to be heard and understood					
Conveying energy, enthusiasm and sincerity in the performance					
Using appropriate facial expressions in the performance					
Using appropriate physical gestures in the performance					
Displaying the text or pictures from it effectively					
Inviting audience participation and interest					

Conclusion

	1	2	3	4	5
Effectiveness in summing up the performance					
Appropriateness for the work presented					

3.5 ORGANIZING A NEWSCAST PROJECT

GUIDING QUESTION 3: How can I demonstrate my new organizing skills?

SUBJECT AREAS: Social Studies

GROUPING: Whole class, cooperative groups

MATERIALS: Video tape of a newscast
VCR/monitor

BLOOM'S TAXONOMY LEVEL: Knowledge, Application, Synthesis, Comprehension, Analysis

PRODUCTS AND OUTCOMES: Plans for a student newscast

TIME FRAME: 3 class periods

Procedure:

Pre-Class Preparation: Make a videotape of a half-hour national or local news show.

Period 1

1. Tell students that their major project will be to plan and present a half-hour newscast. Show the videotape of the newscast you have prepared, telling students to be alert to how the show is organized.

2. Discuss the newscast with the students, having them name its major components—international, national, local news, sports, features, etc. Have them reach consensus on the elements they want in their newscast.

3. Divide the class into cooperative groups, one for each component of the newscast. Let each group meet and decide what it wants to present on the newscast and how much time its segment will take. Each group should select who will meet with those from other groups for planning purposes.

Period 2

1. While groups research, write, and begin to prepare graphic materials for their segments, you, as executive producer, should meet with the group representatives to coordinate time allotted to each segment to ensure that the newscast fits within the allotted half hour.

2. Representatives return to the groups to give the final time allotments and to continue developing the segments.

Period 3

1. Groups should complete drafts of their segments.

2. Representatives should meet and prepare a final plan for the order and timing of the various segments.

EVALUATION:

Students should be able to analyze the organization of a televised newscast.

Students should be able to plan out the contents of their own newscast.

3.6 PRESENTING A STUDENT NEWSCAST

GUIDING QUESTION 3: How can I demonstrate my new organizing skills?

SUBJECT AREAS: Social Studies

GROUPING: Whole class, cooperative groups

MATERIALS: Student scripts, graphic materials, and props such as globes, pointers, maps, etc.
Video camera (optional, if you wish to tape the performance)

BLOOM'S TAXONOMY LEVEL: Knowledge, Application, Synthesis, Comprehension, Analysis

PRODUCTS AND OUTCOMES: Presentation of the student newscast

TIME FRAME: 3 class periods

Procedure:

Period 1
Student groups should work on presentation of materials they developed in the last activity. Each group should decide what role each member will play during the "telecast"—i.e., anchor for the segment, field correspondent, interviewee, graphics coordinator, etc. Tell students that they should continue to revise and edit their material as they begin to rehearse their roles.

Period 2
Groups should come together and jointly work on coordinating production of the newscast. They must make sure that all groups understand the order of the show's sequence, that each group is able to arrange its members and materials efficiently on stage, that segues between different segments of the newscast work efficiently, and that students understand and are comfortable with all tasks they will have to perform during the broadcast. You may wish to allow another period for whole-class rehearsal if you feel it is necessary.

Period 3
Students assemble and present the newscast in one uninterrupted flow. You may, if you wish, invite an audience of "viewers" to the presentation or you may wish to videotape the performance for later critiquing by students.

EVALUATION:
Students should be able to organize, rehearse, and perform their assigned roles in a class-produced newscast.

EVALUATING THE PROJECT

Evaluating My Performance
Check the box that best describes how well you carried out each item below when working on the project.

Performance area	Exemplary	Developnig	Accomplished	Emerging
I used my organizational skills on this project.				
I completed my tasks on time.				
I helped other students.				
I did the best work that I could.				

Thinking About Organization
Think about the part your organizational skills played in this project. Write your responses to the following questions on the lines provided.

In what area was your planning most effective?

_____

_____

_____

_____

_____

In what area could you have planned better?

_____

_____

_____

_____

_____

_____